UNIQUE ANIMALS OF THE
MIDWEST

By Tanya Lee Stone

BLACKBIRCH PRESS

An imprint of Thomson Gale, a part of The Thomson Corporation

THOMSON

GALE

Detroit • New York • San Francisco • San Diego • New Haven, Conn. • Waterville, Maine • London • Munich

For the unique Segal family in the Midwest!

For more information, contact
Blackbirch Press
27500 Drake Rd.
Farmington Hills, MI 48331-3535
Or you can visit our Internet site at http://www.gale.com

Photo Credits: pages 3, 7 (both), 10, 15, 18 (both), 18, 19, 22, 23 (top) Corel; pages 5, 13, 17 Photodisc; pages 6, 14 © Darrell Gulin/CORBIS; page 8 Allen Blake Sheldon (top); © Joe McDonald/CORBIS (bottom); page 9 Allen Blake Sheldon; page 11 © Doug Wechsler; page 12 © D. Robert and Lorri Franz/CORBIS; page 20 © Richard Thorn/Visuals Unlimited; page 21 AP/Wide World Photos; page 23 © W. Perry Conway/CORBIS (bottom)

LIBRARY OF CONGRESS CATALOGING-IN-PUBLICATION DATA

Stone, Tanya Lee.
  Unique animals of the Midwest / by Tanya Lee Stone.
    p. cm. — (Regional wild America)
  Includes bibliographical references and index.
  ISBN 1-56711-965-4 (hard cover : alk. paper)
  1. Animals—Midwestern States—Juvenile literature. I. Title II. Series: Stone, Tanya Lee. Regional wild America.

Printed in the United States of America
10 9 8 7 6 5 4 3 2 1

Contents

The Midwestern United States

Lake Superior

MINNESOTA

WISCONSIN

Lake Huron

★
St. Paul

Lake Michigan

★
Madison

MICHIGAN

★
Lansing

Lake Erie

IOWA
★
Des Moines

INDIANA
★
Indianapolis

OHIO
★
Columbus

ILLINOIS
★
Springfield

MISSOURI
★
Jefferson City

Across the Midwest, birds fly, marine life swims, and animals travel across the land. Many different animals make their homes here. Some animals are especially well known in this region.

A red fox is one of the many animals that make their home in the Midwest.

With bright red patches on the tips of its wings, a male red-winged blackbird is more colorful than a female (left). Red-winged blackbirds live in large flocks (right).

The cardinal and red-winged blackbird live in many parts of the United States. However, the red-winged blackbird is one of the most common birds in the Midwest. And the cardinal is the state bird of Ohio, Indiana, and Illinois.

The male red-winged blackbird is all black except for bright red patches on the tips of its wings. The red patches are often bordered by yellow. The female is not as colorful as the male. It is dark brown and can have some red on its wings. Both the male and female have sharp, pointed beaks. This bird eats mostly seeds and some insects. It uses its beak to crack open hard shells and to spear insects. Red-winged blackbirds are social birds that live in large flocks.

The cardinal male is also brightly colored. It is red all over, except for some black around its bill and neck. Like the female red-winged blackbird, female cardinals are less colorful than males. They are a grayish color with some red patches. Both males and females have a large crest of feathers on top of their heads. Their bills are red, large, and cone-shaped. They have long tails. Cardinals like to eat insects, fruits, and seeds.

A bright red male cardinal brings food to its young.

Totally Turtles!

Many kinds of turtles spend a lot of time in or near water. They are common in the Midwest, which is full of lakes, marshes, rivers, and streams. The blanding's turtle lives mainly in the Midwest region and Quebec, Canada. It can

A blanding's turtle looks like it is smiling (above). A painted turtle (below) shows off its colorful markings while perched on a log.

also be found in parts of Nova Scotia, Nebraska, and New England. It is threatened or endangered in several midwestern states.

The blanding's turtle prefers to live near marshes. It is known for its long yellow neck and for its face, which looks as though it is smiling. This turtle

also has a longer tail than many turtles. It is sometimes hard to spot a blanding's turtle because it hides as soon as it senses danger. This turtle can pull itself completely inside its shell when frightened.

Another common turtle in the Midwest is the painted turtle. It is Michigan's state reptile. This turtle is named for the colorful markings on its shell, neck, legs, and tail. The painted turtle has a fairly flat shell. It can use its shell to hide, but it is harder for the turtle to breathe in this position. Painted turtles like shallow, calm water with muddy bottoms. They eat insects, plants, and small animals.

The common map turtle also lives throughout most of the Midwest. It is named for the pattern of lines on its shell, which looks a little like a map. These turtles prefer deep waters where they can dive to find food and safety. They like to eat snails, crayfish, and clams.

The pattern on the shell of the common map turtle looks like the lines on a map.

Frog Fanfare

The northern spring peeper frog lives in much of the eastern half of the United States and Canada. They prefer woodlands near water and are very common in the Midwest region. The northern spring peeper eats small insects. This tiny frog grows to just over an inch long. It is easy to identify because of the X-shaped marking on its back.

This frog gets its name from the "peep, peep, peep" sound it makes in the spring, or late winter. In the cold winter months, northern spring peepers hibernate. They can tolerate freezing temperatures. A sugary substance in their body called glucose keeps their bodies from freezing. As the weather warms, these shy little peepers begin to be heard.

A northern spring peeper frog is only about an inch long, small enough to sit on a plant leaf.

Only the males sing. A male has a large vocal sac under its chin. The frog puffs the sac full of air, and then pushes the air out, making the peep sound. A large chorus of male peepers can often be heard singing together. Their calls are made to attract mates.

After mating, females lay eight hundred to one thousand eggs. They lay them either singly or in groups of two or three, attaching them to plants in the water. The eggs hatch within four to six days. Tadpoles develop into young frogs over two to four months.

A male peeper fills the vocal sac under his chin with air and then pushes the air out to make a song to attract mates.

A badger shows the white stripe that begins at the tip of its nose, goes over its head, and sometimes goes all the way down to its tail.

Burrowing Badgers

Badgers are related to weasels and skunks. Like skunks, badgers can release a strong scent when threatened. Badgers live in many parts of North America. Wisconsin, though, is known as the Badger State. Badgers are short, strong, stocky animals. They weigh between 25 and 35 pounds (11 to 16 kg). They are usually between 15 and 30 inches (38 and 76 cm) long. A badger's tail is 4 to 6 inches (10 to 15 cm) long.

A badger has a unique triangle-shaped face. Its throat and chin are white, and it has black patches on its face. Its pointy nose is black. A white stripe usually goes from the nose over the back of its head and down to its shoulders. Sometimes this stripe extends all the way to its tail.

Badgers are nocturnal. This means they are mainly active at night. They eat some kinds of plants. They also eat snakes, birds, and reptiles. But their favorite foods are ground-dwelling rodents such as rats, gophers, and mice. Badgers are good at digging and catch most of their food this way. A badger can spot a mouse and follow it, digging holes into the ground right after it. Badgers have strong front legs, and their front paws have sharp curved claws. This helps them dig. Badgers will burrow into the ground to escape attackers, too.

Badgers also dig burrows for sleeping, storing food, and giving birth. These burrows can stretch 60 feet (18 m) into the ground! Badgers will also take over abandoned burrows or holes of other animals. Badgers usually live alone, except when females are raising their young.

Badgers come out at night to hunt for rodents such as rats, gophers, and mice.

Gathering Geese

Snow geese migrate (travel) great distances during the year. During the summer, these birds breed in the Arctic. Then from August to October, snow geese begin migrating to either the Gulf Coast or Mexico. During their journey south, more than five hundred thousand snow geese usually stop to rest and feed in DeSoto National Wildlife Refuge in Missouri. They can be seen stopping in a few other places in the Midwest, and also in the Dakotas.

Snow geese fly fast—between 50 and 60 miles (80 to 97 km) per hour! That's as fast as people often drive their cars! They also travel very high, flying about 3,000 feet (915 m) above the ground. These birds usually migrate in large groups of between one hundred and many thousands.

Snow geese are large birds, standing 28 to 29 inches (71 to 74 cm) tall. They weigh between 5 and 6 pounds (2 and 3 kg). Their strong wings stretch 56 to 60 inches (142 to 152 cm).

Snow geese migrate from the Arctic to Mexico each year, and can fly up to sixty miles an hour (below). The flock occasionally stops to rest and eat.

Darling Deer

The white-tailed deer is well named. Its tail is brown on top with white edges. The underside of the tail is white. A deer will flash the white part of its tail to send a danger signal to other deer. This is called tail flagging. It is also used to help baby deer (fawns) follow their mothers through the forest.

The white-tailed deer lives in many parts of the United States. It is a very common sight, though, in the Midwest region. In fact, the white-tailed deer is the state mammal of four midwestern states—Illinois, Michigan, Ohio, and Wisconsin! Deer like to live in areas that have both meadows and woodlands. They have large home ranges. Deer are herbivores, or plant eaters. They eat shoots, buds, leaves, and stems. They also nibble on nuts and fruit. In winter, they eat bark and tall brush. Deer will dig under snow to uncover any food they can find.

A white-tailed deer sends a danger signal as it flashes the white part of its tail to other deer (above). A baby deer nibbles on the leaves and stems of bushes (below).

Deer are gentle, shy animals. Female deer (doe) and fawns often live and feed together in small groups. Male deer (bucks) also form small groups of their own. White-tailed deer have excellent senses of sight, smell, and hearing. They know when a threat is near and are swift runners. White-tailed deer move quickly to stay out of danger. This helps them survive.

With their excellent senses of sound, sight, and smell, deer are able to sense danger close by.

The thirteen-lined ground squirrel lives in a large area in the middle of the country. This area includes all of the states in the Midwest region. The thirteen-lined squirrel is named for the thirteen alternating brown and white lines that run the length of its back and sides. Inside the dark lines are rows of white spots. This squirrel is between 6 and 11 inches (15 and 28 cm) long.

Squirrels are rodents. Like all rodents, they have front incisor teeth that keep growing. To keep these teeth worn down, squirrels constantly gnaw on hard foods such as nuts and seeds. The thirteen-lined squirrel likes to eat grasses, too. It also eats grasshoppers and caterpillars. Like all squirrels, it has an excellent sense of smell and good eyesight. It also has a sharp sense of hearing.

A thirteen-lined ground squirrel has rows of brown and white stripes that run the length of its body.

A squirrel is most active on warm days and constantly gnaws on hard foods like nuts and seeds.

Squirrels are diurnal. That means they sleep at night and are active during the day. The thirteen-lined squirrel is most active on warm days. It does not like the cold. This squirrel often enters its nest in October and stays there until March or April. During this time it stays rolled up in a tight little ball. Its breathing slows down to conserve energy. When the weather warms up, out it comes again!

Bring Back the Bats!

The Indiana bat lives in five states in the Midwest region. This bat looks much like the common little brown bat. It can be identified, though, by its pink lips. The Indiana bat is an endangered animal. That means it is in danger of becoming extinct.

In the winter, Indiana bats hibernate in caves. They are very social animals. They gather in large groups, packed closely together. These bats used to stay all winter in caves in Indiana and Illinois, but they no longer spend time there. This may be because of more human activity in the caves, which disturbs the bats. Today, most of these bats spend winter in caves in Tennessee and Kentucky. When the weather turns warmer, though, the bats return to the Midwest. They gather under the loose bark of dead trees.

When the weather gets cold, Indiana bats hibernate deep inside a cave.

Bats are unlike any other kind of mammal. That is because they are the only mammal that can fly! Bat wings do not have feathers like bird wings. Their wings are made of a thin skin. The skin begins at the ankles and stretches out over a bat's long fingers. The Indiana bat has a very small body. Its wings, though, span 9 to 11 inches (23 to 28 cm).

Like other bats, Indiana bats make high-pitched sounds that humans cannot usually hear. These sounds hit objects and then bounce back to a bat's ears—like an echo. The echoes tell the bat where an object is. They also tell the bat how big something is and how fast it is traveling. This amazing talent is called echolocation. It makes bats very efficient hunters! Indiana bats mainly feed on flying insects.

The endangered Indiana bat is very small, but has a wide wing span.

Wandering Wolves

Gray wolves once lived in most parts of the United States. Today, about seven thousand live in Alaska. Outside of Alaska, the largest number of gray wolves in North America lives in Minnesota. They are also scattered in states such as Michigan, Wisconsin, and Montana. Gray wolves are threatened in Minnesota. This means they are close to becoming endangered. Everywhere else in the United States, except Alaska, gray wolves are endangered.

Gray wolves can weigh up to 150 pounds (68 kg). They stand about 26 to 32 inches (66 to 81 cm) tall. They live in social groups called packs. There are generally two to twelve wolves in a pack. A pack is usually led by a breeding pair, with the male in charge. The rest of the pack is made up of the pair's pups, and other nonbreeding wolves. Pups are born blind and deaf. They are raised in the safety of a den for the first six to eight weeks. The whole pack helps take care of the pups.

A pack usually hunts together, too. They often go after animals larger than they are. These include deer, elk, or cattle. Wolves also kill small animals such as beaver and rabbit. Together, the pack chases an animal down and attacks until the victim is too weak to fight back.

Wolves communicate with each other by howling, barking, and growling. They also make faces and change the way they stand to send signals to each other. Wolves mark their territory with their scent to warn other wolves to stay away.

There are many unique and wonderful animals that live in the Midwest. All of them add to the richness and beauty of this region.

A six-week-old gray wolf pup (below) is almost ready to leave the safety of its den to join a pack and learn to hunt (above).

Glossary

Diurnal Asleep at night and active during the day.
Echolocation Locating objects using echoes.
Herbivore An animal that eats mainly plants.

Nocturnal Active at night and asleep during the day.
Omnivore An animal that eats plants and other animals.
Pack A group of wolves.

For More Information

Gunzi, Christiane. *The Best Book of Wolves and Wild Dogs.* New York: Larousse Kingfisher Chambers, 2003.

Hickman, Pamela. *Bird Book.* Toronto: Kids Can Press, 2000.

Jacobs, Lee. *Deer.* San Diego, CA: Blackbirch Press, 2002.

————. *Squirrels.* San Diego, CA: Blackbirch Press, 2002.

Stone, Tanya Lee. *Turtles.* San Diego, CA: Blackbirch Press, 2003.

Index